BART

HOMER

MARGE

LISA

MAGGIE

It's wild. It's hilarious.
It's fun. It's . . .

SIMPSON FEVER!

An unofficial fact and quiz book

Now, see how much YOU really know about the hottest television show on this side of the planet! Learn all about the entire Simpsons craze in this handy, easy-to-check-out fact and quiz book! Who knows? You may end up knowing more about the wacky world of the Simpsons than Bart himself!

SIMPSON FEVER!

An unofficial fact and quiz book

JEFF ROVIN

ST. MARTIN'S PAPERBACKS

Simpson Fever! is an unofficial fact and quiz book. Neither the Fox television network, nor any other individuals or companies responsible for The Simpsons, has in any way sponsored, approved, endorsed or authorized this book.

SIMPSON FEVER!

Copyright © 1990 by Jeff Rovin.

ISBN: 0-312-92502-6

Printed in the United States of America

St. Martin's Paperbacks edition/September 1990

10 9 8 7 6 5 4 3 2 1

Acknowledgments

The author would like to express his appreciation to the following for their help in creating this book:

Shep Boucher
Maureen J. O'Neal
Ryan Quirk
Sally Richardson
John Rounds
David Kaye

Introduction

Here's a little stumper to start things off.

Think hard: what do these people have in common with our pal Bart Simpson?

> Orenthal James
> Louis
> Wallis
> Jim

If you don't know, we're not going to tell you—yet. You'll find the answer buried deep in this book. (Actually, it's not buried *too* deep. It's right after the Introduction, as a matter of fact).

In addition to *that* bit of trivia, this book will provide you with hundreds of other incredible facts, details, and questions about America's most popular TV family.

But before we delve into our overview of *The Simpsons*, there's one question we should try to answer up front: why is this brawling, wacky-looking family so popular? Let's face it: if you lived next door to a household with a Neanderthal-like dad, a troublemaking kid, and three utterly unpredictable ladies, do you think you'd be very fond of them?

Probably not.

But that's the magic of TV. Watching it, we step outside of ourselves for a little while and live the lives of the characters on the screen. And living life alongside the Simpson family is appealing for a number of reasons.

For one thing, they're funny.

On Sunday night, with a tough new week about to start, we can all use a good laugh. And since we're not about to get that from *60 Minutes*, *The Simpsons* fills the bill. Also, some of us are a little too sophisticated for the dumb humor of *America's Funniest Home Videos*. (What would Bart think of *America's Funniest Home Videos*? He probably wouldn't be happy with the stuff they show: too tame. He'd want to stage a video, and nothing less than a nuclear meltdown or a flood.)

For another thing, we like the show because Bart and Lisa Simpson are hip. Especially Bart. His language, his appearance, even his modes of transportation are cool without being obnoxiously trendy. He's his own person.

But most importantly, *The Simpsons* is a hit because it hits back. It acknowledges, in living color, what we always knew: that those happy, compassionate TV families run by the likes of Ozzie and Harriet, Donna Reed, and Robert Young were a buncha baloney.

The truth is, parents aren't always even-tempered and they don't always do the right thing. Also, real-life families bicker, just like the Simpsons. Some have members who are burping slobs, like Homer. Some have know-it-alls, like Lisa. Most have lovable brats like Bart (ever notice the similarity between "brat" and "Bart"?)

Yet, through all the turmoil and trouble, the Simpsons stick together—a family to the end. And the message of the show is clear: if there's hope for them, then there's hope for us all. We can learn from *The Simpsons*.

Which brings us back to this book.

The purpose of this book is to tell you everything there is to know about the Simpsons, about the life and works of their creator, Matt Groening, and about other precocious TV and comic strip kids. The more you know about the craze and its origins, the better you'll understand why *The Simpsons* is a cultural phenomenon.

The information in *Simpson Fever!* comes at you in three forms:

- Quizzes, with the answers in the back of the book
- Small chapters on different aspects of the Simpsons rage
- Sections entitled *Fast Facts*, which give you important behind-the-scenes or historical information in neat, little paragraphs. (In fact, the paragraphs are *so* concise, we'll bet that even Bart wouldn't mind reading them! Especially since a lot of them are about him.)

We guarantee you'll have fun wandering through these pages, and we also guarantee one thing more: by the time you've finished reading, you'll hold a very special Ph.D.—a Papa Homer Doctorate.

Have fun, Simpsonsite!

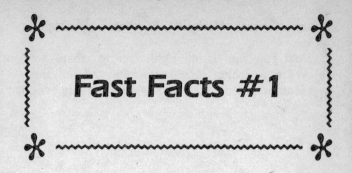

Fast Facts #1

You guessed it, right?

Those first names in the Introduction all have one thing in common: the last name of Simpson.

The difference, of course, is that unlike Bart, the rest of the Simpsons are real.

Orenthal James Simpson—better known as O.J. Simpson—is the legendary football star who played for the Buffalo Bills from 1969 to 1977, then went to the San Francisco 49ers for a pair of seasons. He's also been in movies, TV commercials, and has worked as a sportscaster. Jim Simpson is also a sportscaster, host and/or announcer on shows like *NBC Sports in Action* and *Monday Night Baseball.*

Louis Simpson is an American poet and novelist, while Wallis Simpson is the late Duchess of Windsor, the American woman England's King Edward VIII abdicated the throne to marry.

And in case you were wondering—while no one named Simpson ever got close to the White House (thank heavens!), there *was* Herbert Hoover's secretary of state (and Franklin Roosevelt's secretary of war), Henry L. Stimson . . . which is close!

(Now you can march right over to where your folks are watching *thirtysomething* and tell them you learned something *really* useful from this book!)

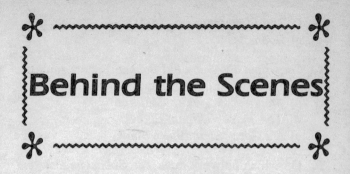

Behind the Scenes

How much do you know about the broadcast history of your favorite show, and about the people and network which spawned it?

1. When did *The Simpsons* debut?
   a) December 31, 1989
   b) January 14, 1990
   c) February 4, 1990

2. Executive Producer James L. Brooks has won three Academy Awards. For which film did he win them?
   a) *Broadcast News*
   b) *Kramer vs. Kramer*
   c) *Terms of Endearment*

3. Brooks was also a co-creator and/or writer on which three of the shows below?
   a) *The Mary Tyler Moore Show*
   b) *The Cosby Show*
   c) *Taxi*
   d) *Gunsmoke*
   e) *All My Children*

f) *The Flintstones*

g) *Room 222*

4. On which TV show did the short-short subject cartoons featuring the Simpsons first appear?

a) *Married . . . With Children*

b) *The Tracey Ullman Show*

c) *It's Garry Shandling's Show*

5. On which network does *The Simpsons* air?

a) ABC

b) FBC

c) NBC

d) CBS

6. Matt Groening and James L. Brooks are two of the three executive producers on *The Simpsons*. Who is the third?

a) Sam Simon

b) Tracey Ullman

c) Jennifer Tilly

7. Name the former *Saturday Night Live* regular who occasionally contributes voices to the show.

a) Harry Shearer

b) Billy Crystal

c) Jim Belushi

8. What well-known prime-time TV star has also done voices for supporting characters?

a) Sally Struthers

b) Roseanne Barr

c) Penny Marshall

9. What is the name of the studio which does the animation for the show?
a) Hanna-Barbera
b) Klasky-Csupo
c) Toei Animation

10. What was the name of the Simpsons special which aired just prior to the debut of the series?

11. Before the debut of *The Simpsons*, which of these shows aired on Fox in the 8:30–9:00 time slot?
a) *21 Jump Street*
b) *Married . . . With Children*
c) *America's Most Wanted*

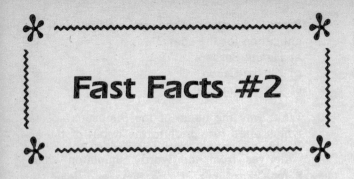

Fast Facts #2

Shakespeare wondered, "What's in a name?" Matt Groening must've wondered the same thing when he named each of his Simpsons.

Here's what the names mean:

Homer:

Greek for "Promise" (which Homer Simpson definitely has little of). Homer, of course, is the Greek poet who wrote the epics *The Iliad* and *The Odyssey*. Obviously, all that he and Homer Simpson share is their name.

Marge:

a familiar form of the name "Margaret," the name comes from the Greek and means "Pearl." No doubt that's why she wears 'em!

Bart:

from the Hebrew, meaning "Son of a farmer." We all know that the only thing Bart ever grows is *bored*.

Lisa:

a familiar form of the name "Elizabeth," the name comes from the Hebrew meaning "Oath of God." Oath, as you know, can be a vow . . . or a curse!

Maggie:

Same as Marge.

As for the family name of Simpson, the root word "simp" derives from the word "simpleton" and means "fool."

Need we say more?

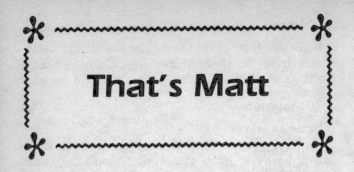

That's Matt

Here's a fun way to learn about the life and times of the creator of *The Simpsons*, Matt Groening.

1. Where was Matt born and raised?
   a) New York, New York
   b) Los Angeles, California
   c) Portland, Oregon

2. When Matt was a child, he won a short story contest in a 1962 issue of which magazine?
   a) *Highlights for Children*
   b) *Jack and Jill*
   c) *Weekly Reader*

3. What was the name of the political party Matt founded in high school?
   a) Teens for Decency
   b) Kids Against Korruption
   c) No War No More

4. Which college did Matt attend?
   a) Cooper Union
   b) Evergreen State College
   c) Northwestern University

5. What was the name of the campus newspaper edited by Groening?
a) *Cooper Point Journal*
b) *The News Rustler*
c) *Today*

6. What is the name of Matt's wife?
a) Deborah
b) Marge
c) Leslie

7. The Groenings' first child was born on March 23, 1989. His name is:
a) Homer
b) Jacob
c) Matt Jr.

8. In 1977, Matt created a syndicated comic strip. Its name was:
a) *Calvin and Hobbes*
b) *Life in Hell*
c) *A Guide to Life*

9. Where do the Groenings presently reside?
a) British Columbia
b) Tucson, Arizona
c) Venice, California

10. Matt's interest in cartooning was encouraged by his father, named:
a) Lou
b) Stan
c) Homer

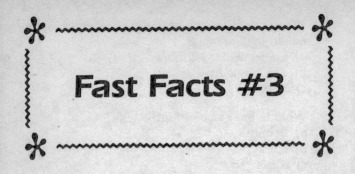

Fast Facts #3

It's Bart's favorite, most oft-used expression: "Aye, caramba!" But do you know what it means? (More importantly, does Bart? If not, hope he's reading this.)

Both are Spanish exclamations. "Ay" (not "Aye") means "Alas," and "Caramba" means "Good gracious" or "Good heavens!" So, while "Aye, caramba" is kind of redundant, it *does* very effectively communicate the despair Bart feels when he utters it.

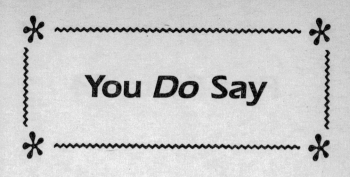

You *Do* Say

Match the voices to the characters:
1. Nancy Cartwright
2. Dan Castellaneta
3. Julie Kavner
4. Yeardley Smith

a. Lisa
b. Marge
c. Homer
d. Bart

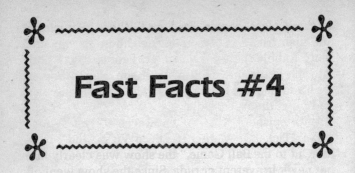

Fast Facts #4

In all of the reviews and articles about *The Simpsons*, two other cartoon series keep popping up: *The Flintstones* and *The Jetsons*.

The reason for this is twofold. First, the two Hanna-Barbera productions were prime-time animated series, and there have been very few of those. (Why? Because adults watch TV at night, and most grown-ups don't consider cartoons suitably sophisticated entertainment. Obviously, they never heard of Jay Ward or Chuck Jones.)

Second, and more significantly, *The Flintstones* and *The Jetsons* were both shows about families—families which were typical of the way the media presented the home during the years when the shows were popular. In other words, the families were wholesome, supportive, and never, *ever* fresh to one another.

How long do you think Bart would have lasted in those series?

Inspired by the live-action series *The Honeymooners*, *The Flintstones* originally aired from September, 1960, to September, 1966. The half-hour show was about the adventures of the prehistoric working class couple Fred and Wilma Flintstone, and their friendly, blue collar neighbors Barney and Betty Rubble. Later, a daughter, Pebbles, was born into the Flintstone clan, while a son, Bamm Bamm, was adopted by the Rubbles. The Flintstones also had a pet dinosaur, Dino.

With episodes like "At the Races," "The Sweepstakes Ticket," "Mother-in-Law's Visit" and "Take Me Out to the Ball Game," the show was clearly fun, but never irreverent or rude. Since the show went off the air, the characters have been seen in countless other series, mostly on Saturday mornings, ranging from *Pebbles and Bamm Bamm* to *Fred and Barney Meet the Thing,* the Thing being the Marvel Comics superhero of the same name. Talk about whipping a property until it's black and blue: could anything dopier have been done with poor Fred and Barney? (Probably . . . but it's too painful to contemplate!)

As for *The Jetsons,* they've become cult figures . . . though they were never as popular, in their initial run, as *The Flintstones.* Since the Flintstones were a cave family, it was only logical to make the Jetsons a space-age family, living in the year 2062. Airing from September, 1962, to September, 1963, the show starred George and Jane Jetson, teenage daughter Judy, son Elroy, dog Astro, and the robot maid Rosie. Once again, with adventures like "The Flying Suit," "A Date With Jet Screamer," and "Dude Planet," there was nothing terribly bizarre.

Incidentally, it's a little-known fact that Hanna-Barbera tried two other family cartoon series: *Roman Holidays* and *These Are the Days. Roman Holidays* was about Gus and Laurie Holiday, their daughter Precocia, their son Happius, and their pet

13

lion Brutus. This show was actually as much fun as the previous series, but audiences had had enough of cartoon family antics and it only lasted from September, 1972 to the following September.

These Are the Days was somewhat more serious, being the life and times of a family living at the turn of the century: widow Martha Day, her husband's father Jeff Day, and Martha's children Ben, Cathy, and Danny. It ran from September, 1974 to September, 1976.

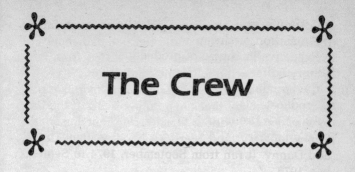

The Crew

These are the people who do all the nitty gritty work on *The Simpsons*, from making sure the show stays within budget, to overseeing the writing of the script, to making sure the artwork is up to snuff.

Your task: match the person with the title she or he holds on *The Simpsons*.

If you sit by your TV set at the end of the show, and watch closely, you'll be able to figure this one out. A VCR with a "pause" feature will be even handier.

1. Margot Pipkin
2. Richard Sakai
3. Jon Vitti
4. Bonnie Pietila
5. Antonia Coffman
6. Michael Stanislavsky
7. Craig Knizek
8. Larina Adamson
9. Al Jean
10. Mike Reiss

a. Co-producer
b. Fox press contact

c. Co-producer
d. Animation producer
e. Executive in charge of production
f. Story editor
g. Casting director
h. Producer
i. Associate producer
j. Co-producer

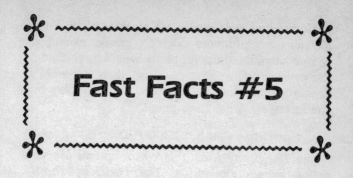

Fast Facts #5

In the last Fast Facts, we told you about *The Flintstones* and *The Jetsons*. Here's an overview of some of the other animated families which have appeared on TV, though not in prime-time:

The Barkleys:

this was another cartoon show inspired by a live action series, in this case *All in the Family*—only it didn't feature humans, it starred dogs! Arnie Barkley was a bigot, Agnes was his long-suffering wife, and their children were Terri, Chester, and Roger. The show aired from September, 1972 to September, 1973.

The Brady Kids:

a series based on the prime-time live-action series about a widower and widow who marry and combine their families. It ran from September, 1972 to August, 1974.

The Gerald McBoing-Boing Show:

this character actually began as the star of movie shorts, and came to TV in December, 1956: his show went to prime-time during the summer of 1958. Gerald was a child who couldn't speak, except for "boing" sounds. (Bart probably would have thought that was neat, at first . . . and then it would've driven him wacky!) Gerald lived with his folks in a comfortable middle-class home.

Partridge Family: 2200 A.D.:

like *The Brady Kids,* this was a spinoff of a live action prime-time series, *The Partridge Family.* However, there was one small difference: Shirley Partridge and her kids Keith, Laurie, Danny, Tracy, and Chris were based on the Earth of the future! It ran from September, 1974 to March, 1975.

Walt Till Your Father Gets Home:

a show in which the old-fashioned father, Harry, is out of sync with the rest of his family—wife Irma and children Alice, Chet, and Jaimie. The half-hour Hanna-Barbera show was offered for syndication in the fall of 1972.

Where's Huddles:

another Hanna-Barbera series, this one focusing on the home life of quarterback Ed Huddles, his wife Marge, and their neighbors Bubba and Penny McCoy. It aired for two months, beginning in July, 1970.

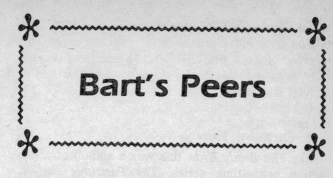

Bart's Peers

Like any character, Bart Simpson wasn't created in a vacuum. He's part of a long stream of characters that have appeared in TV shows—some of them good guys, some of them considerably less than good. If you can believe it, in his day, one of these guys—Little Ricky Ricardo—was even *more* famous than our pal Bart!

In the list below, you'll find famous TV characters who were either Bart's age and/or young pains in the butt. Match the characters to the series in which they appeared.

1. Chip Lowell
2. Opie Taylor
3. Ritchie Petrie
4. Arnold Jackson
5. Little Ricky Ricardo
6. Alex Keaton
7. Theodore Huxtable
8. Dennis Blunden
9. Eddie Haskell
10. Jonathan Bower

a. *The Cosby Show*
b. *Leave it to Beaver*

c. *The Andy Griffith Show*
d. *The Dick Van Dyke Show*
e. *Head of the Class*
f. *Who's the Boss*
g. *Kate & Allie*
h. *Diff'rent Strokes*
i. *I Love Lucy*
j. *Family Ties*

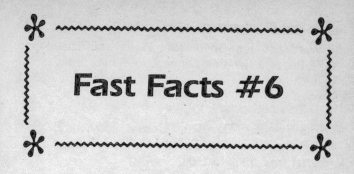

Fast Facts #6

In addition to talking about classic cartoon families, reviews and commentary about *The Simpsons* have compared the show to live-action series about families.

You're probably familiar with the most popular families on TV today: the happy Huxtables, battling Bundys, and cranky Conners of *The Cosby Show, Married . . . With Children* and *Roseanne,* respectively.

Back in the 1950s and 1960s, though, TV families consisted of wise, patient adults and precocious, impish, but generally good and respectful kids. Here's a guide to the most popular of those families:

The Andersons:

Jim and Margaret (popular mom's name, huh?), with kids Betty (aka Princess), James (aka Bud), and Kathy (aka Kitten). Seen on *Father Knows Best* from 1954 to 1963.

The Cleavers:

Ward and June, with kids Wally and Theodore (aka Beaver). Seen on *Leave it to Beaver* from 1957 to 1963.

The Nelsons:

The legendary Ozzie and Harriet, and sons David and Ricky. Starred on *The Adventures of Ozzie and Harriet* from 1952 to 1966.

The Stones:

Dr. Alex and Donna, and kids Mary and Jeff. The perfect family seen on *The Donna Reed Show* from 1958 to 1966.

The Williamses:

Danny and Margaret (again! . . . though she later "died" and was replaced by Kathy), and progeny Rusty, Terry, and Linda. Seen on *Make Room for Daddy* (later called *The Danny Thomas Show*) from 1953 to 1971.

Other sunshiny families, not as well-known as these big five, include the Hendersons of *Beulah* (1950 to 1953), the Bumsteads of *Blondie* (1957), the Roses of *Room For One More* (1962), the Baxters of *Hazel* (1961 to 1966), and the Collinses of *The Bing Crosby Show* (1964 to 1965).

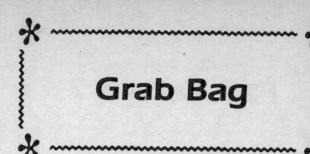

Grab Bag

1. How many fingers do the Simpsons have on each hand?

2. In what color dress is Marge usually seen?

3. How much does it cost to make an episode of *The Simpsons?*
   a) $300,000
   b) $700,000
   c) $1 million

4. True or false: Homer's boss frequently calls him "mush mind."

5. What is the name of the bowling alley seen in the series?
   a) Barney's
   b) Bernie's
   c) Bennie's

6. Super-toughie: what size shoe does Marge wear?

7. True or false: According to Marge, the secret to being popular is to wear Elizabeth Taylor's Passion perfume.

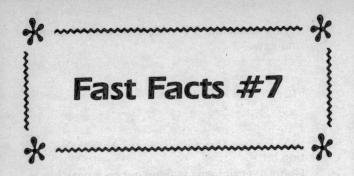

Fast Facts #7

Before Bart came along, easily the most troublesome character the media had ever seen was Dennis the Menace.

When cartoonist Hank Ketcham was trying to come up with a new cartoon strip, he didn't have to look any farther than his own four-year-old son. *Dennis the Menace* made its debut as a one-panel newspaper comic on March 12, 1951, and is still going strong.

Dennis is the son of Henry and Alice Mitchell—decent, middle-class folks who watch with alarm as Dennis terrorizes their elderly neighbors, Mr. and Mrs. Wilson, and also—are you ready for yet another one?—his young schoolmate Margaret. As Mr. Wilson sums up Dennis's antics, "Henry and Alice must dye their hair. Otherwise they'd both be *gray!*"

Don't take Mr. Wilson's word for it—see for yourself. Among Dennis's more outlandish achievements, misdeeds, and observations have been:

- Using his mother's bra to make a tail for a kite.
- Making a chocolate cake sandwich for lunch.
- Breaking out his drum set shortly before dawn.

- Trying to fix the TV with a crowbar, hammer, and saw.
- Referring to his mom's tapioca pudding as "fish eyes and glue."
- Threatening to kill himself if his father doesn't buy him a color TV.
- Refusing to have his big dog stop slobbering over a guest, insisting that it's better than getting bit.
- Going over to teens making out on a park bench and trying to convince them they'll have more fun playing baseball with him.
- Demanding in a loud voice at a Chinese restaurant, "What are these little things that look like spiders next to those little things that look like worms?"
- Commenting sourly at a birthday party, "I don't call a lousy rubber ball *first prize!*"
- Voicing this philosophy to his pal Joey: "You shouldn't go home the minute your mother yells. You'll *spoil* her!"

Dennis was played by Jay North in the popular TV series which ran from 1959 to 1963.

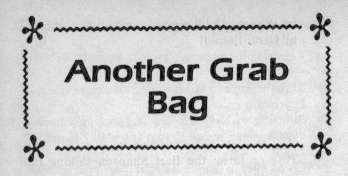

Another Grab Bag

1. Which one of these operas was featured in an episode of the show?
   a) *Carmen*
   b) *The Magic Flute*
   c) *Aida*

2. Which one of these magazines has *not* featured the Simpson family on their cover?
   a) *TV Guide*
   b) *Newsweek*
   c) *Good Housekeeping*

3. How many episodes of *The Simpsons* were produced for the show's first season?
   a) 13
   b) 17
   c) 22

4. Name the comedienne who has offered to provide the voice of Maggie when the baby learns to speak:
   a) Lily Tomlin

b) Whoopi Goldberg
c) Carol Burnett

5. By April of 1990, how many Simpsons T-shirts were selling every week?
   a) 10,000
   b) 100,000
   c) one million

6. True or false: the Bart Simpson talking doll belches.

7. Which toy company makes the Simpsons figurines?

8. In his top-selling poster, Bart warns us to keep out of his:
   a) Face
   b) Room
   c) Way

9. True or false: Bart once had a dog named Flea.

10. True or false: Bart plays Gin Rummy with his father every Sunday night.

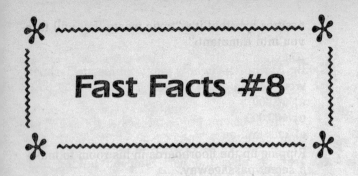

No discussion of currently popular troublemaking boys can possibly be complete without mentioning Calvin, one of the great comic strip pests.

Created by Bill Watterson and introduced in the *Calvin and Hobbes* strip in November of 1985, the six-year-old boy has only one true friend: his stuffed tiger Hobbes, who is a real live animal as far as the boy is concerned.

Hobbes is actually a mitigating factor in the youngster's life, constantly counseling him as to what he should and shouldn't be doing.

Not that Calvin ever heeds the tiger's advice, which results in such questionable acts as:

- Standing by as nemesis Susie Derkins passes, and shouting at her, "I hope you suffer a debilitating brain aneurism, you freak!" (And people say *Bart* is rough on his enemies!)
- Announcing in the school cafeteria that he's having "a squid eyeball sandwich" because he likes "to suck out the retinas."
- Digging up the entire yard to make speed bumps for himself.
- Agreeing to eat his dinner only after his father

assures him that it's "toxic waste that will turn you into a mutant."

- Asking his dad why he lives with a wife rather than with several scantily clad females.
- Refusing to take a math test, arguing that it's against his religious beliefs.
- Trying to get rid of his father using the TV remote control.
- Ripping up the floorboards in his room to make a secret passageway.
- Suggesting to his stressed-out father that he go into a line of work other than parenting.

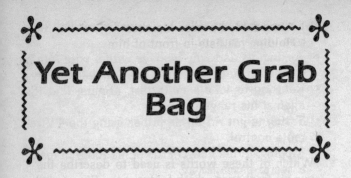

Yet Another Grab Bag

1. True or false: Bart once won a spelling bee by spelling the word "skateboard."

2. True or false: Bart's middle name is Herbert.

3. True or false: there is a file in the principal's office just for Bart.

4. True or false: the Indiana Department of Transportation wants Bart to appear on official road caution signs.

5. True or false: Matt Groening has a mother named Marge, and sisters named Maggie and Lisa.

6. True or false: Homer has been known to strangle family members.

7. How is Bart standing in the famous poster featuring him in his superheroic identity?
   a) Hands on his hips

b) Arms folded across his chest
c) Holding his fists in front of him

8. According to a popular button featuring Bart, he is not at all ashamed to be:
a) An underachiever
b) A straight-F student
c) A skateboarder

9. Which of these words is used to describe the car air freshener which features the Simpsons?
a) Odorable
b) Scentsational
c) Smellerific

10. How long does it take for an episode of *The Simpsons* to go from idea to finished product?
a) Two months
b) Six months
c) Nine months

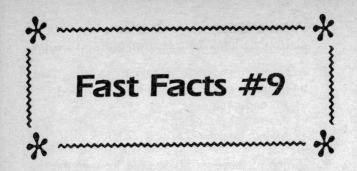

Fast Facts #9

As you can imagine, when there's a hit like *The Simpsons,* it means that other producers are going to be jumping on the bandwagon.

Not long after it was clear that the show was a smash, other prime-time, half-hour animated series were announced.

The first was a show starring that old warhorse the Pink Panther. Introduced in the opening credits of the film *The Pink Panther* in 1964, he was subsequently spun off into a highly successful series of theatrical cartoons, and about a zillion different TV series. One of the more recent such incarnations was *The Pink Panther and Sons* in 1983, which gave the fantastic feline two sons: Pinky and the impish Panky. Presumably, the new show will feature his family as well.

Another series looking to duplicate the success of *The Simpsons* is actually a cross between the Groening show and Teenage Mutant Ninja Turtles: it's *The Jackie Bison Show,* the story of a talk show host who is also a buffalo.

Others which are in the planning or production stages for prime-time:

Aristocritters,

a political satire about mice who live in the White House.

Danger Team,

the story of a bookkeeper who becomes a private investigator. This one will use clay figures, a la Gumby.

Family Dog,

a cartoon series inspired by an episode of the otherwise terrible *Amazing Stories*.

Fish Police,

based on the absolutely terrific comic book of the same name about—you guessed it!—crimebusting fish who live in a fully developed fish society.

Except for the fish, we think we'll stick with Bart and Company.

Mind-Blowing Trivia Challenge

If you've been able to answer most of the questions till now, try these on for size:

1. What animals are in the window of the pet shop during the opening titles?
a) Dogs and cats
b) Birds
c) Fish

2. Also during the titles, what is visible on the multiple TV screens in the store window as Bart whizzes by?
a) Krusty the Clown
b) Denzel the Dog
c) A Springfield Subsonics basketball player

3. How many bicycles are visible in the garage *before* Lisa gets home?
a) None
b) One
c) Two

4. What's unusual about the wall to the right of the sofa in the living room?

a) There's a mouse hole in it
b) Bart's drawn a moustache on a photo of his sister
c) There's dried food stuck to the wall

5. What can be found between the brick wall and the garage at the side of the Simpson house?
a) A broken-down motorcycle
b) A clothes line
c) Trash cans

6. What is Marge's full first name?
a) Margaret
b) Marjorie
c) Margenia

7. What color is "The Simpsons" during the opening credits?

8. What film company produces the show in association with Twentieth Century–Fox Television?

9. In what year did the Simpsons make their TV debut as fifteen–twenty second shorts?

10. What props up the short leg of the sofa in the living room?
a) A telephone book
b) A dictionary
c) A block of wood

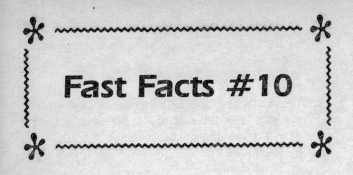

Fast Facts #10

One of the most unusual events involving the Simpsons was held on April 28 in New Brunswick, New Jersey: it was a Simpsons lookalike contest, held to benefit St. Peter's Medical Center.

Entrants paid $2 and vied for more than $200 in prizes. Seems a pretty skimpy reward for coming forward and *admitting* that you look like one of the characters. Fortunately, the cause was a worthy one.

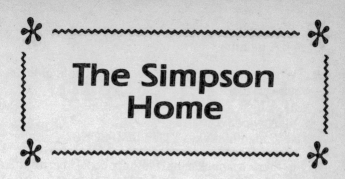

The Simpson Home

1. Next to the living room sofa is a table which has two objects. What are they?

2. True or false: there are three trees in the front yard.

3. What color are the kitchen tiles?
   a) Red and black
   b) Green and yellow
   c) Blue and white

4. True or false: the Simpsons own a baby grand piano.

5. Is there a fireplace in the Simpson home?

6. True or false: there's a grandfather clock in the foyer.

7. There's a mirror and table to the right of the door in the foyer. What's to the left?
   a) A coat rack

b) A lamp
c) A painting

8. What is located directly over the outside of the garage door?
a) A light
b) A window
c) A sign that says "THE SIMPSONS"

9. Is there a knocker on the outside of the front door?

10. What is located to the right of the TV?
a) A lamp
b) A plant
c) A rocking chair

11. Is there an aerial on the TV?

12. Where is the door to the basement located?
a) In the kitchen
b) In the side of the staircase leading to the second floor
c) Inside the garage

13. Here's a real braincruncher: how many steps lead down to the basement?
a) Six
b) Nine
c) Fifteen

14. True or false: A broken metronome is sitting on top of the piano.

15. True or false: A dishwasher is to the left of the telephone.

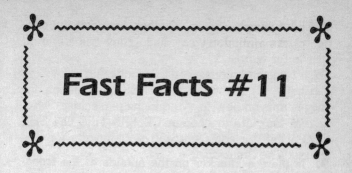

Fast Facts #11

On a less happy note than the fund-raising we talked about in our last FAST FACTS, is this: Bart is being frowned upon in some schools!

Imagine—our hero, our academic wizard being bounced from classrooms.

The T-shirt on which Bart boasts of being an underachiever, and another in which he utters the word hell have been banned at the Cambridge Elementary School in Orange, California.

The underachiever shirts have been nixed at five schools in Fremont, Ohio.

"That's not exactly the type of behavior we hope elementary schools model," says Cambridge principal Jamie Brown.

Bet no one would've complained if a kid came in wearing a shirt showing a sports figure or movie star who'd been busted for drugs. Or Samuel Taylor Coleridge, the brilliant poet who was also an opium addict.

Or wearing a Wile E. Coyote garment. (He only tries to kill the Road Runner using boulders, TNT, and other delightful items.)

Or wearing shirts showing such fine role models

as Eddie Murphy, Slash, or other distinguished public figures who don't say hell. They use *different* four-letter words.

Isn't kneejerk conservatism wonderful?

(Check out our SELF DEFENSE KIT section for suggestions on how to avoid being persecuted! Also, have a look at our chapter CELEBRITIES ON THE SIMPSONS for some perceptive comments for and against *The Simpsons*!)

Celebrities on *The Simpsons*

Here are exclusive, never-before-published comments about Bart, his family, and the phenomenon of *The Simpsons* from a wide variety of world-famous celebrities:

> "I don't know much about Bart Simpson, but the theme of the irreverent child is nothing new. Romeo didn't listen to his parents, either."
> —Charlton Heston,
> star of *The Ten Commandments* and *Ben-Hur*

> "I'm not sure the so-called negative impact of Bart Simpson is as strong as people seem to fear. Even a powerful post-hypnotic suggestion given to a receptive subject lasts only a day or two and then it's forgotten. The only time a suggestion lasts longer is if it's reinforced.
>
> "Without reinforcement from the parents, telling the kids to follow this or that; and without constant reinforcement from peer groups, a thing called *boredom* will set in. And if that happens, even the most ferocious stimuli will become a thing of the past. I can remember, as a kid, being told that hysterical,

overly-emotional behavior would come from attending performances of a singer named Frank Sinatra. Well—we all survived."

—The Amazing Kreskin,
mentalist

"Role models do have some impact, I'll grant you. My son, when he was five, came to me in tears one day because he hadn't saved anyone from danger the way his hero Superman had.

"As for negative influences, there's so much in our society and culture which glorifies goodness that a balance is inevitably struck. Think back to the Grouch on *Sesame Street.* How many kids who saw that went out to live in a garbage can?"

—George Plimpton,
author

"My feeling is that we're concerned about one tiny tessera in an enormous mosaic of mediocrity. We're living in a climate of ignorance. We need a revolution in education, and I'm not hopeful that we'll get it. In that sense, *The Simpsons* won't make a difference one way or the other."

—Tony Randall,
actor

"I have to admit, it doesn't seem like a bright idea having a show where the parents are dull and the youngsters are wisecrackers. I would say this to parents: don't worry about things like this unless you see it becoming an obsession—like with the Teenage Mutant Ninja Turtles, where there were kids who went climbing around in sewers. Otherwise, it will pass, like all things."

—Maureen Stapleton,
Oscar-winning actress

"It's stupid of the kids to wear those (Simpsons) shirts to school. Jesus Christ, our whole system's gone to hell! We *should* have control over what kids wear to school. I object to all this because it's anti-learning. We've got a nation of kids who don't read, and who *can't* read, and we're worried about hurting their feelings? Anyone who thinks that underachieving is funny, in any context, is stupid."

—Ray Bradbury,
author

"I have no problem with a show that's disrespect-ful, as long as the child is taught that other people have the same freedoms that he has—for example, that adults have the freedom to disagree with what he's doing. But every child has to find his own voice, and often he has to go through a season of disrespect to do it.

"I don't think that we should be overly concerned with disrespect, but rather, with violence in the me-dia. Violence tells kids there's only one solution to a disagreement, which, obviously, is wrong. Compared to that, the furor over what a kid wears on his T-shirt is inconsequential."

—Robert Lansing,
actor

"I wouldn't say that just *The Simpsons* are to blame, but I think there's a lot of justified concern about the types of shows our children are seeing on television. Everything is written and performed with such a low level of manners and grace. It's crazy— and I don't know if we can pull back to when things were more pleasant to watch.

"I'll tell you this much, though. I don't think there would be all this concern about *The Simpsons* or *Married . . . With Children* or any of the other shows if the parents of today's children would spend more time at home. You can't be an absentee parent. You can't leave kids in front of the tube, not discuss with them what they've seen, and then blame the television for all of our problems."

—Helen Hayes,
actress

"I think *The Simpsons* is absolutely brilliant and beautifully done—the art is unique, the scripts well-written, and it's compelling and amusing, a good job all around.

"As for the harm it's supposed to be doing—young people are much more sophisticated than most of the 112 so-called experts give them credit for. The furor over the T-shirts is silly. Anyone who's old enough to know what 'underachiever' means understands that it's meant in a satirical way.

"I feel, overall, that if there were more humor in our lives, more shows like *The Simpsons*, we might be doing better as a society."

—Stan Lee,
comic book writer and creator of
Spider-Man and the Incredible Hulk

"I'm not altogether discouraged to see shows like *The Simpsons* in vogue. I meet kids in the military who are nineteen and they're great, just sharp and smart as can be. I'm not worried that they're going to become underachievers because of a cartoon character."

—Wally Schirra,
Mercury, Gemini and Apollo astronaut

"I think the show's a lot of fun. All this talk about it being bad for kids—that's just not so. They said the same thing about *Batman,* that the violence was a bad influence, that the villains were bad role models. Kids aren't dumb. They know when something is supposed to be taken with a grain of salt. The first time a young boy dresses as a ninja, takes a hacksaw, and cuts the head off a giant bronze statue in the town square, I'll be awfully surprised.

"I have to mention, though, that I do take some pride in the fact that we were doing those same tilted camera angles on *Batman* that they're doing now on *The Simpsons.* It's nice being ahead of your time!"

—Adam West,
TV's *Batman*

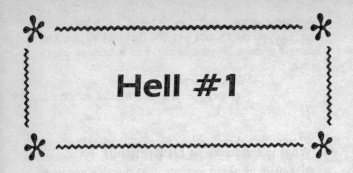

Hell #1

Before he was masterminding the misadventures of the Simpsons, Matt Groening was drawing the comic strip *Life in Hell*, which served as the basis for his many cartoon books. Indeed, it looks like he'll be writing books for quite some time to come: earlier this year, Groening signed a seven-figure contract with a publisher which entitles them to fifteen new projects.

Our concern, in the HELL sections, is with Groening's previous works, comic strip and books alike.

If you don't know much about them, and if you love *The Simpsons*, stop reading *this* book right now. Go out and buy all the Groening books you can find, read 'em, and then try these quizzes.

1. The book *Greetings from Hell* is a book which consists of:
   a) Postcards featuring Groening characters
   b) A map of hell
   c) Autobiographical essays by Groening

2. What is the name of the star of *Life in Hell*?
   a) Winky

b) Stinky
c) Binky

3. What kind of animal is he?
a) A human
b) A rabbit
c) A mouse

4. What is the name of his girlfriend?
a) Zinky
b) Queenie
c) Sheba

5. What is the name of his illegitimate son?
a) Ralph
b) Gulliver
c) Bongo

6. What is unusual about this offspring?
a) He has only one ear
b) He only speaks in rhymes
c) He wants to be an opera singer when he grows up

7. Co-starring in the strip are Akbar and Jeff. They are:
a) Lawyers who turn down cases which offend their sense of morality
b) Brothers or lovers, and may be both
c) Siamese twins

8. One of the most famous Groening cartoons warns that if you drink, you shouldn't:
a) Drive

b) Drill
c) Draw

9. Akbar and Jeff opened a restaurant known as Tofu Hut. What was it previously called?
a) Weenie Barn
b) Cholesterol City
c) Bran Loyalty

10. According to a Groening chart, which one of these is closest to the primordial ooze whence all life sprung?
a) Baboons
b) Two truck drivers
c) Young Republicans

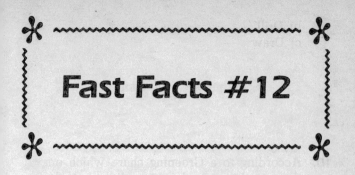

Fast Facts #12

The composer of the theme song for *The Simpsons*, Danny Elfman, is fast becoming one of the world's most important figures in orchestral music!

Believe it or not, Elfman began his career as the leader of the rock group Oingo Boingo, with which he still plays.

Elfman got into movie scoring when he was tapped by his friend, director Tim Burton, to compose the music for Burton's feature film debut, *Peewee's Big Adventure* in 1985. He gained greater fame with his soundtrack for Burton's hit movie *Beetlejuice*, but it was his driving, somber score for *Batman* that really put him over the top . . . and high on the record charts. Since then, he's also done the score for *Dick Tracy* and the theme music for the hit HBO series *Tales from the Crypt*, among others.

With *The Simpsons*, Elfman told *Billboard* Magazine, "We all wanted to go for the classic feeling in the tradition of *The Flintstones* and *The Jetsons*, with a lightweight, modern approach." However, he added that because of his own preference for "horror and the macabre," some appropriately sinister overtones found their way into the music.

Springfield

1. One of the local radio stations is KBBL. What do the call letters stand for?

2. True or false: TV 6 covers the town of Springfield.

3. What is the name of the founder of Springfield?
   a) Jebediah Springfield
   b) Roscoe Simpson
   c) Lewis N. Clark

4. The abovementioned is famous for having helped the local settlers survive:
   a) The great flood of '45
   b) The great blizzard of '48
   c) The mosquito infestation of '51

5. True or false: the Simpsons worship at the Drive-In Church of Springfield.

6. What is the name of the local movie theater?
   a) The Springfield Palace

b) The Megamulticineplex-seventeen
c) The Aztec

7. Where in Springfield can you buy delicious-to-drink Squishies?
a) Kwik-E-Mart
b) Squishies 'R' Us
c) 8-12

8. True or false: the name of the retirement home located in Springfield is called Geezer Farm.

9. Where's the best place to buy candy in Springfield?
a) Sweeney's Sweets
b) Candy Most Dandy
c) Hard Rock Candy

10. True or false: the mayor of Springfield is named Mayor Dinkie.

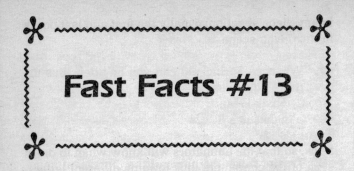

Fast Facts #13

How, exactly, does an episode of *The Simpsons* go from an idea to a finished show?

Like this:

The producers, writer, and story editor get together and hash out ideas. When they've hit on a suitable story line, the writer goes home and creates the script.

When that's done, everyone reads it, puts in their two cents, and the writer makes revisions, if necessary. After that, copies are sent to the actors.

A rehearsal follows, in which the actors work on different kinds of delivery, different inflections, different tones. For example, a line might be tried as a kind of whispered aside, or said sarcastically, or through clenched teeth. If the actors come up with any suggestions for new or different lines, those are occasionally incorporated into the script.

When the rehearsal period is finished—usually after a day or two—the actors go into the recording studio. The voices are taped, after which the tape and script are sent to the animation studio. There, a crew of approximately fifty artists does two thousand pencil drawings which show the *main* events in any piece of action: usually the first and last poses in any given scene.

These drawings are then sent, with the tape, to a studio where "in between" work is done: that is, pencil drawings which fill in the action between those two thousand illustrations done previously. Before these can be drawn, of course, special breakdown sheets have to be done of the vocal soundtrack, so that the animators will know when to draw each of the characters' lips forming different letters.

The finished cartoon will consist of approximately 16,000 drawings.

These drawings are done on paper, and are then transferred to transparent sheets known as cels. This transferral process can be done one of two ways: by laying the cel over the pencil sketch and tracing it onto the cel using ink (this is costly and time-consuming), or by using a process known as Xerography, where the pencil sketches are photocopied onto the cels. The cels are then hand-colored using paints.

Why is it necessary to transfer the drawings to cels? So that the same background drawing can be used for each picture. If you couldn't see the background through the cel, it would have to be redrawn for each picture. Needless to say, that'd take a loooong time.

When the cels have been inked, and all of the backgrounds drawn, they are placed on an animation stand: a table with a camera overhead. The first cel is placed on the background and photographed on a single frame of film, then it's removed and the next successive cel is put on the background and photographed, and so on. When all the frames are shown in succession, it looks as if the characters are alive . . . much like the figures in a flicker book seem to move when you flip the pages.

When the cartoon has been photographed, the composer writes the music, the sound effects people put in various clunks, slams, and crashes, and the half hour masterpiece is ready to air!

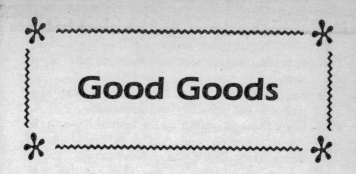

Good Goods

You already know about the poster in which you're admonished to stay out of a certain kid's room (you've bought over a quarter of a million of them).

And you know about the buttons with their various slogans.

And the quadrillions of T-shirts. And the talking Bart doll, and the Simpsons "action" figures.

If you've got those, and are in the mood to add to your collection, here are some other ultra-cool Simpsons things you can buy:

- Workout clothes: from leggings to big T-shirts to sweat socks, you'll be the talk of the gym. (It's a little bit of a contradiction having the un-fit Simpsons on exercise clothes . . . but why be a party pooper?)
- Watches: you absolutely *must* have the digital watch with the pop-up faces of the characters. If you can't get this, go for the analog watch with the portrait of the family.
- Party favors: requisite stuff for any party, the goods here include hats, horns, plates, napkins, and tablecloths.

- Sheets: don't know about you, but we'll sure sleep better on sheets, pillowcases, bedspreads, and comforters featuring the Simpsons.
- Keychain: time to get rid of that Batman keyring and get hip with the Simpsons.
- Gum: this one's gotta be the best of all. In June, Amurol started selling gum in the shape of Bart's head. That's one chewed dude!

We wonder: with all of this merchandise, can Maggie Simpson pacifiers be far behind?

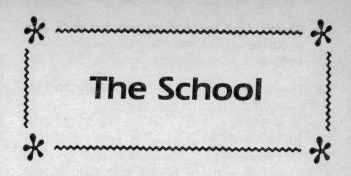

The School

Here's a short section about Bart's favorite place on the face of the planet Earth:

1. What is the name of the school the Simpsons attend?

2. What is the name of the principal?
   a) Mr. Steeler
   b) Mr. Wetherbee
   c) Ms. Noyes

3. What is the name of the school psychologist?
   a) Anna O. Freud
   b) James Pryer
   c) Carl Young

4. What school did Bart briefly attend?
   a) Enriched Learning Center for Gifted Children
   b) Springfield School for the Gifted
   c) Genius Elementary

5. How many pictures are there on the bulletin board in Bart's class?

a) One
b) Three
c) Five

6. How many members are there in the school orchestra?
a) Eleven
b) Twenty-two
c) Thirty-three

7. True or false: the name of the bus driver is Mrs. McGrew.

8. True or false: in one version of the opening, a kid hooks a skull-and-crossbones to the flagpole out front.

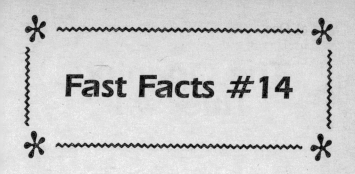

Fast Facts #14

Unless you grew up in the forties or fifties, you may not be aware of the fact that there was a very popular prototype for Homer: a chunky, blue collar family man by the name of Chester A. Riley.

The show was *The Life of Riley,* and it began as a radio show in 1943. The star was William Bendix, who played a hard-hat working at an aircraft factory in California. However, most of the stories were set at home, with the fumbling but good-natured Riley, his wife Peg, their daughter Babs, and their son Junior.

The series came to TV in 1949, but as Bendix was tied up with film roles, Jackie Gleason got the part. He was so wrong as Riley that the show went off the air after just one season. When Bendix was free of other commitments, he agreed to do the series; it was a smash, and ran from 1953 to 1958.

Like Marge Simpson, he tended to mangle words and utter malapropisms. His most famous phrase was, "What a revoltin' development this is!"

The Opening
Titles #1

1. True or false: at the start of the show, the title *The Simpsons* appears from behind a mountain.

2. Here's a toughie: which is the last letter of their name to disappear from the screen?

3. What symbols are visible on the twin cooling towers of the nuclear power plant?

4. There's a pile behind the power plant, to the left. It consists of:
   a) Glowing nuclear rods
   b) Old automobile tires
   c) Old cars

5. True or false: there's a man walking his dog near the nuclear power plant.

6. True or false: the movie theater is visible on the main street.

7. The sign outside the school consists of:
   a) Red letters on a white background

b) White letters on a blue background
c) Blue letters on a yellow background

8. What's the color of Bart's sneakers?

9. There's a notice posted at the checkout counter of the supermarket. It discusses:
a) Checks
b) Coupons
c) Store hours

10. True or false: the dentist's sign on the main street reads Semi-Painless.

11. How many books is Lisa bringing home?
a) Three
b) Six
c) Nine

12. True or false: Marge is riding alone in the car.

13. What is the man doing behind Homer at the plant?
a) Napping
b) Eating a sandwich
c) Turning dials

14. When the names of the show's creators appear in the titles, whose name is the first one seen?

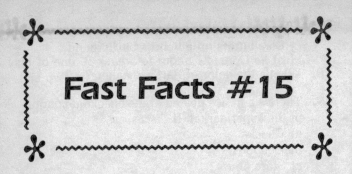

Fast Facts #15

The Simpsons is unusual among cartoon shows because the action in the opening credits changes from week to week in two ways: Bart's always writing something different on the blackboard and, when the family sits on the couch at the end, something different always happens.

But the show isn't the first series to do this!

From 1955 to 1959, ABC aired Walt Disney's afternoon show *The Mickey Mouse Club*. The animated opening of the show would always end with Donald Duck standing beside a gong, ready to bang it. And each time he did, something different would always happen. For instance:

- The gong, when struck, splatters like a large cheese pizza.
- The gong is made of paper and, when Donald strikes it, he goes flying through.
- The gong shatters like glass.
- The Duck hits the gong, but there's no sound. Bewildered, he places his ear to it . . . and *then* it rings, vibrating him like a tuning fork.
- Donald strikes it, and the gong twists like a coin spun on end, slapping his feathered behind over and over.

- Donald's nephews pop up from behind it and shoot him with their water pistols.
- Just as Donald's about to whack it, one of his nephews runs up and hits it with his own mallet, stealing Donald's thunder.

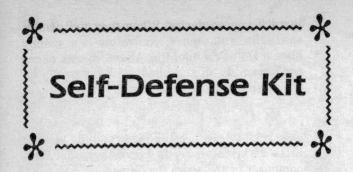

Self-Defense Kit

If you're getting razzed by authority figures because you're wearing a Bart t-shirt, or sporting a Bart button, fear not! Here's some wise-guy trivia you can throw at your adversary to knock them for a loop, and show them that you're no dummy!

- Tell 'em that Bart is no common fool! In fact, ask them if they realized that "bart" is the abbreviation for the noble title "baronet."
- Point out that by insulting Bartholomew Simpson, they're indirectly insulting the entire population of Bartholomew County, Indiana.
- Suggest to them that this is your way of honoring St. Bartholomew, and insist that you just couldn't wait for August 24th, when the annual festival is held in his honor.
- Indicate to your English teacher that you like Bart because he reminds you of that great literary character Lily Bart, heroine of Edith Wharton's 1905 classic *The House of Mirth*. Your teacher will be so shocked you knew this, we guarantee he or she will forget about the Bart T-shirt you're wearing!
- Inform them that you're allowed to wear a

beard if you so desire. When they tell you to stop talking nonsense, you've got 'em: calmly alert them to the fact that "bart" means *beard* in German.

- If you're studying Spanish, you can always claim that the word was "bartulos" (tools), before the other letters came off in the wash.

- In music class, you can blithely tell the teacher that this is your way of honoring Lionel Bart, composer of the score for *Oliver*.

- As a last resort, you can maintain that the name Bart is a subliminal message aimed at them: Be A Righteous Teacher.

Can't Get Enough of those Grab Bags!

1. True or false: when he learned to speak, Bart's first word was "Hey!"

2. What was the name of the newspaper at which Groening worked after graduating from college?
   a) *The Los Angeles Reader*
   b) *The Los Angeles Times*
   c) *Cartoonists Weekly*

3. Which fast-food chain offered cups featuring the Simpson family?

4. What is the average weekly audience for *The Simpsons?*
   a) Ten million viewers
   b) Thirty million viewers
   c) One hundred million viewers

5. *The Simpsons* was based on a novel Matt Groening wrote while he was in high school. What was the name of that seminal novel?
   a) *Mean Kids*

b) *The Tell-Tale Bart*
c) *Caramba!*

6. True or false: if you eliminated his rather high hair, Bart is actually *shorter* than Lisa.

7. Name the candy whose TV commercials feature Bart:
   a) M & Ms
   b) Skittles
   c) Butterfingers

8. True or false: Bart said that if he had a dog, he would name it "Dog Dude."

9. True or false: Lisa's favorite composer is Frederic Chopin.

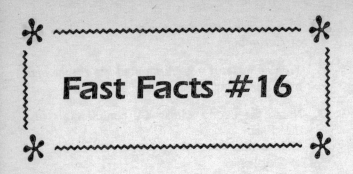

Fast Facts #16

Is *The Simpsons* the most popular show on television?

It might well be!

Unlike ABC, CBS, and NBC, the Fox network does not reach every section of the country. Thus, only about eighty percent of the families with TV can receive it. Despite that fact, it's usually knocking on the door of the ratings top-ten, in spot thirteen or fourteen. And consider how well it'd do if it weren't opposite that powerhouse on ABC, *America's Funniest Home Videos*, and CBS's mighty *Murder, She Wrote*.

If it reached the entire nation, chances are good its ratings would put it on the very top of the list.

The Simpsons is the most popular show on the Fox network, barely beating out *Married . . . With Children*, which follows it.

Other shows which air on the fledgling network (or networkette) are *21 Jump Street*, *Alien Nation*, and *In Living Color* . . . which looks like it's fast becoming a hit as well.

1. What magazine is Marge reading while she waits on line?
   a) *Home Goddess*
   b) *The National Midnight Star*
   c) *Mom Monthly*

2. The advertisement on the back of the magazine is for:
   a) Frosted Krusty Flakes
   b) Happy Elf Videos
   c) Chez Paree Restaurant

3. True or false: the checkout clerk is a woman.

4. What color are the dresses of the twins sitting next to Lisa?
   a) Red
   b) White
   c) Blue

5. True or false: the sign behind Homer at the plant reads "No Smoking."

6. True or false: as Bart leaves the school, Martin Prince waves at him.

7. True or false: a dog hops out of Lisa's way as she hurries home.

8. How many people are waiting at the bus stop?

9. What product is advertised on the side of the bus?
   a) Burpsie Cola
   b) Blubble Gum
   c) Duff

10. What color is the conductor's bowtie?

11. Where do the names of the show's creators appear?
    a) On a wall
    b) On a window
    c) On the TV

12. From left to right, in what order do the Simpsons sit on the couch?
    a) Homer, Bart, Marge, Maggie, Lisa
    b) Marge, Lisa, Maggie, Homer, Bart
    c) Homer, Marge, Lisa, Maggie, Bart

13. True or false: A bee goes down the back of Homer's shirt as he leaves his job.

14. Who wrote the music seen during the opening credits?
    a) Axl Rose
    b) Paula Abdul
    c) Danny Elfman

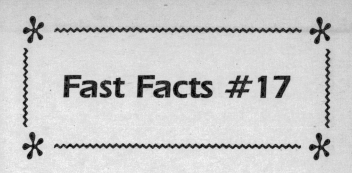

Fast Facts #17

Bart holding public office?

It almost happened.

In a student election earlier this year, Bart won votes at both Stanford University and UCLA. In both cases, he was disqualified *not* because he's a fictional cartoon character, but because he's not enrolled at the schools!

This prompted widespread student protests, which cooled when Bart sent a telegram to the students at Stanford. As quoted by AP, the telegram read, "I must tell you I have set my sights on higher goals. Bart Simpson for U.S. president in '92, man!"

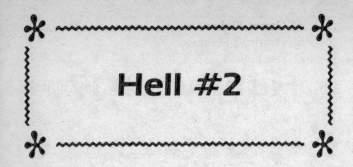
1. Which *four* of these titles are *not* a part of the book series?
   a) *Love is Hell*
   b) *Childhood is Hell*
   c) *Marriage is Hell*
   d) *Death is Hell*
   e) *Work is Hell*
   f) *School is Hell*
   g) *Hell is Hell*
   h) *Homework is Hell*

2. What kind of hat do Akbar and Jeff wear?
   a) A fez
   b) A beret
   c) A derby

3. Who lives across the street from Binky?
   a) Weird Wally
   b) Crazy Fat Lady
   c) Wolf Gang

4. What brand of breakfast cereal is eaten in the Binky household?

a) Carrot Flakes
b) Dandruff Flakes
c) Fun Flakes

5. What was the name of Akbar and Jeff's airport restaurant?
a) Airport Snack Bar
b) Fly Me to the Muenster
c) Plain Food for Plane Folks

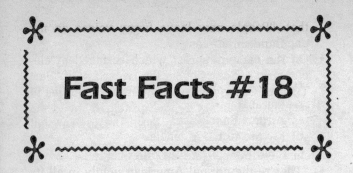

Fast Facts #18

What does Matt Groening think of the show and its popularity? Here are some quotes which have appeared in Groening interviews and press releases:

- "They're an hallucination of a sitcom."
- "Basically, *The Simpsons* are a middle-of-the-road American family in the Midwest who, because they're animated, can be much wilder than live-action families."
- "I don't think of it (the show) as being dark. I do what I think is funny."
- "The world kicks Homer in the ass but he doesn't resent it. And that's because he doesn't *get* it."
- "In many ways I think our show is less cartoony than many live-action shows."
- A nuclear power agency complained about having a numbskull like Homer working at a power plant. Groening says, "They said we're confusing and frightening the American public. *We're* confusing and frightening the American public?"
- One sideshow aspect of his success, he says, is

that, "People now leave funny voices on my phone machine."

- On the campus unrest which surfaced at elementary schools over the wearing of Bart T-shirts, Groening says, "My folks taught me to respect elementary school principals, even the ones who have nothing better to do than tell kids what to wear."

Executive Producer James L. Brooks adds:

- "They're the normal American family in all its beauty and all its horror."

And Tracey Ullman, whose show first featured the characters in snippets, wryly says this of the more popular spinoff:

- "Next season, we're going to appear as a live, 30-second spot on *The Simpsons*!"

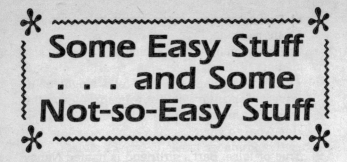

Some Easy Stuff . . . and Some Not-so-Easy Stuff

1. There's a basket hanging in the kitchen, right behind Homer's seat. What's in it?
   a) Flowers
   b) Apples
   c) A stack of dish towels

2. True or false: in the reception area of the power plant, the public can pick up a pamphlet entitled, *Where To Run In Case of a Meltdown.*

3. What's the name of the safety inspector at the power plant?

4. True or false: Marge Simpson moonlights as a gas station attendant.

5. What number do you dial to reach the blustery, insensitive radio psychologist, Dr. Monroe?

6. What is the name of the superheroic identity of Bart Simpson pictured on posters and buttons?

7. What is Bart's full first name?

a) Barton
b) Bartram
c) Bartholomew

8. True or false: in one episode of *The Simpsons*, Bart snuck out of the house and went to see a movie called *Ohio Smith and the Last Band-Aid*.

9. True or false: Bart's girlfriend is named Nancy Joseph.

10. Which one of these is *not* a local newspaper tabloid in The Simpsons' home town?
a) *The Springfield Weekly*
b) *The National Informer*
c) *The Global Tattler*

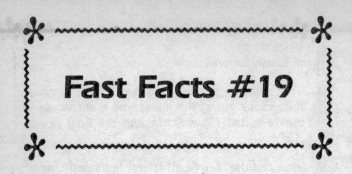

Fast Facts #19

How did *The Simpsons* go from being short sketches on *The Tracey Ullman Show* to having its own series?

According to viewer mail, there was a lot of interest in the characters. Barry Diller, the chairman of Fox, decided to do four specials featuring the characters. However, when he saw an unfinished version of the first show, the Christmas special, he was blown away.

"It's not often I've had . . . the experience of watching something great and praying that the minute doesn't dash it," he says.

But the excitement didn't fade as he continued watching the rough cut. Feeling that the characters had the potential to catch on in a big way, Diller dropped the plans to make a series of specials. He told the producers to go ahead and make thirteen episodes of *The Simpsons*, and scheduled it as a regular series on the network.

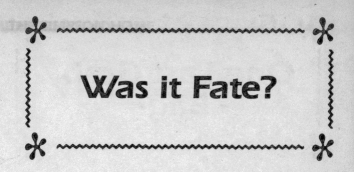

Was it Fate?

Here's a strange coincidence for you to ponder.

From 1949 to 1971, *The Ed Sullivan Show* was seen on Sunday nights from 8:00 to 9:00.

In February of 1964, Sullivan had the rock group The Beatles on his TV show. That appearance helped the popularity of the British quartet skyrocket.

In 1983, former Beatles member Paul McCartney helped to nurture the career of a young singer, Tracey Ullman. Her hit single "They Don't Know" introduced her to American audiences.

Thanks to her recording career, Tracey got her own show when the Fox network was founded. The Simpsons were created to appear on her show.

In 1990, *The Simpsons* debuted in their own shows on Sunday evenings . . . smack in the middle of the slot once occupied by Ed Sullivan. Unwittingly, Sullivan had helped to breed his own Sunday night successors!

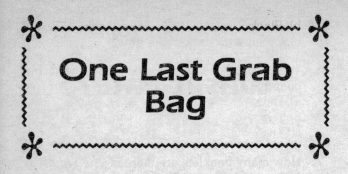

One Last Grab Bag

1. True or false: the name of the Springfield basketball team is the Subsonics.

2. When did the Christmas special air?
   a) December 11
   b) December 17
   c) December 25

3. Fill in the blank: in interviews, Groening has described the series as, "A _____ Ozzie and Harriet".
   a) Modern
   b) Mutant
   c) Mondo

4. According to the talking Bart doll, the kids who watch television are being:
   a) Duped
   b) Dumber than toast
   c) My best pals

5. What color is the kids' toy box?
   a) Red

b) Black
c) Green with dark polka dots

6. Which of these words does Bart most frequently use when he addresses people?
a) Dude
b) Bub
c) Mister

7. How many booklets are there in *The Simpsons Trivia* series from AFCO?

8. Now that *The Simpsons* is being moved to Thursday nights, it will be opposite which of these shows?
a) *The Cosby Show*
b) *Roseanne*
c) *Major Dad*

9. What time did the show air on Sunday evenings (Eastern Time)?

10. Who is the most intelligent member of the family?

. . . Except for *This* Grab Bag

1. What is the name of the bartender seen on the show?
   a) Manny
   b) Moe
   c) Jack

2. During the opening titles, which one of these is *not* visible behind the school building?
   a) Hills
   b) Houses
   c) The sun

3. True or false: the name of one of Krusty the Clown's sidekicks is Sideshow Bob.

4. What is the name of the Simpson family cat?
   a) Snowball
   b) Alley
   c) Clawed

5. What delightful snack sits on the counter at the local tavern?
   a) Jellied grapes

b) Pickled eggs
c) Sugared radishes

6. True or false: there's a TV antenna on top of the Simpson home.

7. True or false: Springfield is the home of the National Kite-Flying Hall of Fame.

8. Who is the worst kid in school?
a) Alvin Capone
b) Alex DeLarge
c) Jimbo

9. True or false: when he was three and went trick-or-treating for the first time, Bart dressed as Santa Claus.

10. True or false: Bart's favorite snack is Twinkle Cakes.

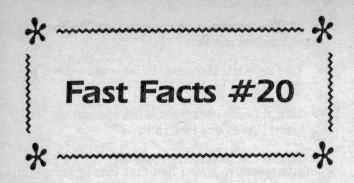

Fast Facts #20

For months, psychologists and educators have been sitting around scratching their heads and pontificating about the appeal of *The Simpsons*.

But what do the kids who watch feel about the show? We asked a few, and here's what they had to say about why it appeals to them, and even what they'd do to improve it:

- "It shows people how they really are, and how they really talk and dress."

  —Victor, age 14

- "It's the only cartoon show for teenagers—except for *Teenage Mutant Ninja Turtles*."

  —Michael, age 13

- "I like it because the kids are smarter than the parents."

  —Samuel, age 10

- "I like it because no one gets hurt, like they do in other cartoons."

    —Rebecca, age 7

- "Me too."

    —Caroline, age 5 (Rebecca's sister)

- "I love the show because I get to stay up late to watch it. I also like that Homer gives Bart money."

    —Aaron, age 9

- "It would be better if they just made one small change: if Bart had a flying skateboard like Marty has in *Back To the Future II*, he'd be truly awesome."

    —Craig, age 14

- "I like the funny faces everyone makes when something bad happens."

    —Kyle, age 6

- "What's good about the show is that Lisa is smarter than Bart. That's true to life, since girls are smarter than boys."

    —Karen, age 7

- "Bart isn't as bad as people think. When he cut off the head of that statue ("The Telltale Head"), he felt guilty."

    —Ryan, age 9

• "I hate school, so Bart is my hero. He does things I'd be afraid to."

—Paul, age 9

• "I don't like it because the drawings are ugly."

—Joshua, age 10

• "I think it's boring. When they thought Homer was Bigfoot, it wasn't realistic."

—Valerie, age 12

• "There's nothing else on, then."

—Eva, age 10

Groening: Art and Scholarship Collide

The evolution of *The Simpsons* is reminiscent of those commercials for Reese's Peanut Butter Cups: two *very* unlikely disciplines crashed head-on to form the family.

Artwise, Groening told an interviewer, "I never thought I was going to be a cartoonist because my drawing ability didn't improve much after the sixth grade." That's the reason, he said, "my characters look alike," with big round eyes, a bulbous nose, and an overbite.

But if his art was raw, his intellectual development was anything but that. In college, he studied a great deal about the Danish philosopher Kierkegaard (1813–1855), who was famous for his bleak outlook on life, his attacks on organized religion, and his criticism of contemporary morality.

Sound familiar?

The combination of the bright, loopy art and downbeat philosophy is one of the qualities which makes *The Simpsons* truly remarkable.

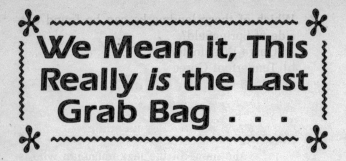

We Mean it, This Really *is* the Last Grab Bag . . .

1. Which word is misspelled in the opening credits?

2. A dream sequence in one cartoon was unusual because it was filmed:
   a) In black and white
   b) Using live actors
   c) Using Claymation

3. Which one of these shows is *not* a series seen on *The Simpsons*?
   a) *The Happy Little Elves*
   b) *America's Most Armed and Dangerous*
   c) *Springfield Tonight With Walter Yenta*

4. True or false: in one episode, the evil babysitter Florence Nightmare comes to watch the kids.

5. True or false: there's a picture of the nuclear power plant behind Maggie's crib.

6. True or false: the Simpsons' telephone number is 555-DORKS.

7. Which of these landmarks can be found outside of Springfield?
a) Gorge Washington
b) Tenderfoot Gorge
c) Gorgeous Gorge

8. True or false: *The Skateboard Decal Catalogue* is Bart's favorite reading material.

9. What is the name of the jazz musician who is Lisa's greatest inspiration?
a) Dexter Gordon
b) Neal Hefti
c) Bleeding Gums Murphy

10. True or false: Bart once began writing a book called *The Allosaurus That Ate My School*.

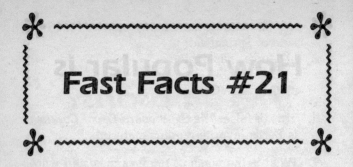

Fast Facts #21

It's a good bet that President Bush will one day refer to Bart in a speech, or that Vice President Quayle will one day quote Homer Simpson when he meant to quote the poet Homer. To date, however, the highest ranking official to make news with a comment about Bart has been drug czar William J. Bennett.

On May 16, while he was touring a drug treatment center in Pittsburgh, he noticed a poster of Bart on the wall and said to recovering addicts, "You guys aren't watching *The Simpsons*, are you? That's not going to help you any."

As if the national drug policy office is, right?

Brad Turell of Fox responded with appropriate restraint: "We have great respect for Mr. Bennett's task and responsibility. But I am not aware of any one TV program that will help teenagers kick the drug habit."

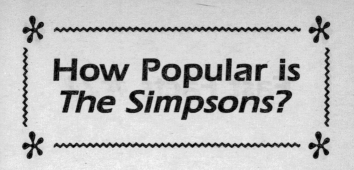

How Popular is The Simpsons?

Here's a list of the hottest toys, shows, movies, fads, and celebrities.

In the blank to the left, write in which one you like the most, second, third, and so forth.

Before this book went to press, we presented the list to over fifty kids, ages 9 through 13 (half were boys, half girls). We averaged the results to find out which are the most popular dudes in the nation! We printed the results in the back of the book. Just for fun, compare their rankings to yours.

_____ Bart Simpson
_____ Batman
_____ Eddie Murphy
_____ Super Mario Bros.
_____ New Kids on the Block
_____ Teenage Mutant Ninja Turtles
_____ Paula Abdul
_____ Pee-Wee Herman
_____ Arnold Schwarzenegger
_____ Chip 'n' Dale's Rescue Rangers

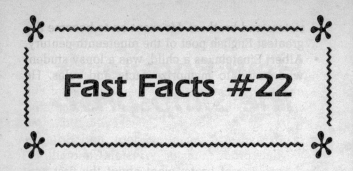

Fast Facts #22

You want to talk about brats?

All the mindless blather about Bart being a bad kid is just that: mindless blather. Look at some great figures who had acts of brattiness or failure in their pasts:

- Michelangelo, the great Italian artist, absolutely *refused* to listen to his parents when he was a child: they wanted him to become a scholar, but he wanted to become an artist. He stubbornly refused to study at school, even though he was severely beaten. Eventually, Michelangelo got his way.
- George Washington, according to popular legend, once picked up an axe when he was a kid and chopped down a cherry tree. Yet, he grew up to be "first in war, first in peace, and first in the hearts of his countrymen."
- Franklin Pierce, the future fourteenth president of the United States, hated school so much that he ran away from it!
- Percy Bysshe Shelley, as an adolescent, used to make up incredible lies about monsters and devils living at his house, and told them to his

sisters and brothers. He went on to become the greatest English poet of the nineteenth century.

- Albert Einstein, as a child, was a lousy student who hated to memorize facts and rules. He eventually became the greatest scientist of this century. Other awful students, incidentally, were George Armstrong Custer (who did a few dumb things as an adult, too), and Britain's wartime prime minister, Winston Churchill.

And speaking of brats, what about the first cartoon featuring that adorable role model for millions, Mickey Mouse? In *Steamboat Willie* (1928), he cruelly played "Turkey in the Straw" by banging on a cow's teeth and pulling her udders, then yanking a cat's tail to get it to scream out musical notes!

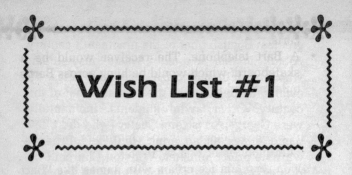

Wish List #1

We asked those same kids we talked to before (along with a few adult fans) the following question:

"What Simpsons product or tie-in would you like to see?"

Some of the answers we got are as follows:

- A book of Bart's funniest sayings or favorite jokes.
- Simpson Cereal or Frosted Krusty Flakes.
- A real videotape with adventures of the Happy Elves.
- A videogame with Bart skateboarding home from school.
- A tape of Lisa playing her favorite songs on the saxophone.
- Videotapes of *The Simpsons* shows.
- A Simpsons comic book.
- Simpsons trading cards with color pictures.
- Bart practical jokes, like leaky pens and pepper-flavored gum.
- A Simpsons amusement park, like Disneyland. Suggestions for attractions include shopping cart rides, a wild trip through a nuclear power

plant, skateboard areas, and saxophone concerts.

- A Bart telephone. The receiver would be a skateboard, which would be hung across Bart's outstretched arms.
- A daily comic strip.
- A live action movie.
- A coloring book *not* of the characters, but filled with pictures drawn by Bart.
- Non-premium ice cream with names like "Bart 'n' Bananas" and "Homer Hash."
- A line of Marge Simpson hats.
- An album of rap songs about the Simpsons.

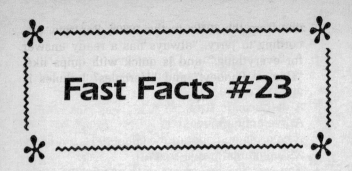

Fast Facts #23

Here's more on Bart's most famous (and infamous) forebears!

Dennis the Menace is the most memorable of the brats who preceded Bart, and Calvin of *Calvin and Hobbes* may be his most famous contemporary, but there have been many other pranksters and pests—especially in comic books.

Here are a few of the most troublesome and/or famous:

- Reggie Mantle: the sly, dark-haired teen has been a nasty rival of wholesome Archie Andrews since *Jackpot Comics* #5 in 1942. Once, he even became the supervillain Evilheart the Great who, armed with a Destructo Ray, tried to blast his nemesis. Even Bart wouldn't go that far!
- Herbie Popnecker: here was a *true* pill. Lazy, snide, and fat, the young teen did little but complain for most of the twenty-three-issue run his comic book *Herbie* enjoyed in the middle 1960s.
- Renfrew: one of the greatest brats of any medium, he was Jerry Lewis's pint-size, slingshot-toting nephew in the 124-issue run of his maga-

zine from the 1950s to the 1970s. Renfrew, according to Jerry, "always has a ready answer for everything," and is quick with quips like, "Dames! Phooey!" and "Hercules? Jerkules is more like it!"

- The G.I. Juniors: four mischievous kids—Tuffy, Chubby, Junior, and Ape—who try to get away with murder at a military school in *Harvey Hits Magazine* during the 1960s.
- Alfred E. Neuman: the mascot of *Mad* magazine has appeared primarily on the cover of that illustrious humor publication, performing various feats of ineptitude and irreverence. He first appeared in issue #21 in 1955.

Note: only the adventures of Reggie and Alfred E. Neuman are still being published. You can find comics featuring the other characters in most well-stocked comic book shops.

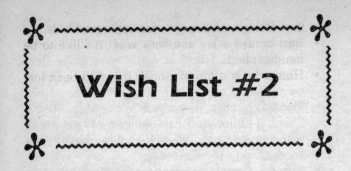

Wish List #2

We also asked our panel of kids and adults what stories they'd like to see on the next season of *The Simpsons*.

Some of their suggestions were:

- Batman or the Teenage Mutant Ninja Turtles come to Springfield.
- Bart's brain is switched to Homer's body, and Homer's brain is switched to Bart's body.
- Bart is made principal for a day.
- A ghost haunts the Simpson home.
- Bart is sent into the future.
- Bart loses his memory.
- Homer quits his job and the Simpsons move to a farm.
- Bart goes to the power plant when there's a meltdown, and becomes a mutant.
- Springfield is taken over by terrorists.
- Bart gets the power to read minds.
- Maggie becomes a giant.
- Homer starts to shrink.
- Bart becomes invisible.
- Bart paints a picture. When an art critic mistakes it for a masterpiece, Bart becomes the toast of Springfield.

- Bart starts a newspaper for oppressed kids.
- Bart breaks a leg and sees what it's like to be handicapped.
- Homer finds a ton of money that had been lost by mobsters and spends it all. Then they come looking for it.
- Lisa wins a musical contest, and is signed to a gig at a local jazz club. Bart is jealous of her success.
- The Simpsons' car breaks down in the middle of a super-bad neighborhood.
- Bart makes a bet with his father that he can be a polite, obedient little angel for twenty-four hours.

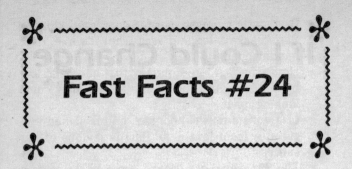

Fast Facts #24

Incredible as it may seem, *The Simpsons* is *not* the first time the name was used for the title of a show.

Back in 1930, there was a radio series called *Snow Village*, which was set in a rustic New England town. Several years later, stars Parker Fennelly and Arthur Allen were spun off in their own dramatic series, *The Simpson Boys of Sprucehead Bay*, which was basically a recycling of the earlier stories.

Nothing like our Simpson family, though.

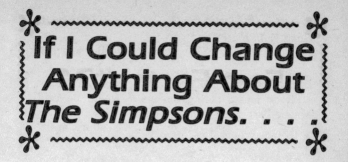

If I Could Change Anything About The Simpsons. . . .

We asked kids and adults what, if anything, they'd change about *The Simpsons*. Here are their replies:

"Since Bart is such an effective role model, I'd have him get involved in anti-smoking and anti-drinking campaigns. That would not only do some good, but it would stop a lot of the complaints aimed at the show."

—David, age 36

"Bart should have a pet dog . . . a tough one, to keep other kids from picking on him."

—Leslie, age 10

"The Simpsons should go to Japan."

—Ken, age 44

"I'd have episodes in which Bart gets to play famous roles from film history, like Marlon Brando's biker from *The Wild One* or Homer and Marge do *Gone With the Wind.*"

—Barry, age 36

"Rock music during the show would be cool. Maybe Bart could form a band."

—Rory, age 13

"I'd like to see Marge start her own business. Unlike Homer, who doesn't have brain one, she has the potential to make something of her life."

—Loree, age 42

"We should see more of the Simpsons' relatives. I know how crazy *my* family is, and we're comparatively normal. Homer's brothers or sisters would be a sight to behold!"

—Matt, age 22

"Flashbacks would be a lot of fun. The family could be gathered around the table, and Homer or Marge could talk about their own childhood or courtship or Bart's babyhood. These could be short segments—about the same length as *The Simpsons* were when they were on Tracey Ullman's show."

—Anne, age 63

"I don't know if they could do this without ruining the show, but I'd like to see the Simpsons win the lottery or inherit a bundle. As funny as they are in suburbia, I think they'd be funnier in the haunts of the rich—private schools, country clubs, that sort of thing."

—Paula, age 38

"I want Bart to learn karate so he can beat up anybody that picks on him. Including his teachers."

—Michael, age 13

"One of the things I hate about cartoon shows is how everyone is frozen in time. I'd like to see the Simpsons age like real people."

—Jim, age 53

"I wouldn't change anything. That would mess it up."

—Chris, age 14

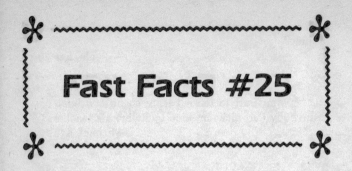

Fast Facts #25

Not only weren't there any Simpsons on the air before Homer and company moved in, but there's been a dearth of Barts on TV as well!

As you read, try to picture Bart Simpson in any one of these roles. . . .

- Bart Adams was the hero of the series *The Hunter,* which aired from 1952 to 1954. He was a businessman whose dealings involved him in all kinds of international intrigue. Barry Nelson, and then Keith Larsen, played the part.
- Bart Matthews was the handsome young attorney seen on *Public Defender,* which lasted from 1954 to 1955. Reed Hadley starred.
- Bart Maverick was the brother of Bret Maverick on the hit western series *Maverick* which ran from 1957 to 1962. Together, the two womanizing, rather cowardly young men got into all kinds of trouble in the Old West. Jack Kelly played the Bart part.
- Bart Stone was the dimwitted young nephew of an industrialist in the comedy *One in a Million.* Richard Paul played the part on the series, which aired in 1980.

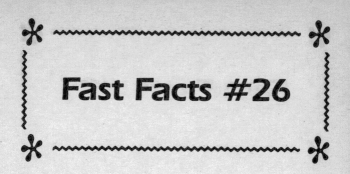

Fast Facts #26

Some quick did-you-knows:

- Springfield was also the name of the hometown in *Father Knows Best*.
- Groening is pronounced "graining"—it rhymes, says a Fox publicist, with "complaining."
- Bart's comic book hero is Radioactive Man— and there really *is* such a character, only he's a villain. He first appeared in Marvel Comics' *Journey Into Mystery* in 1963, as a foe of the superhero Thor.
- Bart's impish habit of calling the bar and asking for people like "Al Coholic" and "Oliver Clothesoff" was also done by some fun-loving lads in the 1981 film *Porky's*.
- Most of the animation art for *The Simpsons* is drawn in South Korea. As you might have guessed, help is cheaper there.

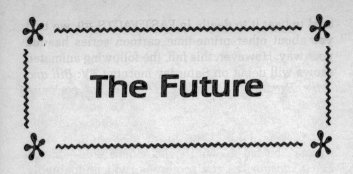

The Future

What lies ahead for Bart and his family?

More controversy, for one thing. According to the industry newspaper *Variety*, many sponsors refuse to air commercials on the show—heavyweight advertisers such as Hershey, Volkswagen, Heinz, Oscar Meyer, Toyota, and others.

Ironically, *The Simpsons* is the top-rated show in the country among 18 to 24 year olds—the age group advertisers *most* want to reach. So it's clear that, despite the unofficial boycott, *The Simpsons* won't be hurting for sponsors.

And the show continues to gain acceptance not just among viewers, but among professionals. For instance, the episode "There's No Disgrace Like Home," involving shock therapy, was so popular among many psychiatrists that they swamped Fox with requests for copies of the show. Educators may have problems with *The Simpsons*, but many, many others do not.

The show will continue to be popular for the foreseeable future, though there *is* the chance that the concept of the precocious kid will wear thin. After all, whenever TV gets hold of a hit concept, they tend to beat it to death. In FAST FACTS #9, we told you about other prime-time cartoon series headed your way. However, this fall, the following animated shows will debut on Saturday morning TV: *Bill and Ted's Excellent Adventure*, starring the cocksure characters seen in the feature film, and *Bobby's World*, featuring Howie Mandel as the obnoxious four-year-old he portrays in his stage act. By 1991, we may be fed up with smart-mouth kids—though *The Simpsons*, as the prototype, will undoubtedly outlast them all.

Regardless of what happens in the future, *The Simpsons'* place in history is secure. It has broken down barriers with its language, expressionistic style, and artistic integrity. Long after the shouting about Bart T-shirts and witless parents has died down, that is what will be remembered.

Answers

BEHIND THE SCENES

1. b
2. c
3. a, c, g
4. b
5. b
6. a
7. a
8. c
9. b
10. *The Simpsons Roasting on an Open Fire.*
11. b.

THAT'S MATT

1. c
2. b
3. a
4. b
5. a
6. a
7. a
8. b
9. c
10. c . . . yes, the same as his son.

YOU DO SAY

1. d
2. c
3. b
4. a

THE CREW

1. d
2. h
3. f
4. g
5. b
6. e
7. i
8. a, c, or j
9. a, c, or j
10. a, c, or j

BART'S PEERS

1. g
2. c
3. d
4. h
5. i
6. j
7. a
8. e
9. b
10. f

GRAB BAG

1. Four. Just like the toes! And, for that matter, just like the eye-lashes on each eye of the female members of the family.
2. Green
3. b
4. False
5. a

6. 13AA
7. False

ANOTHER GRAB BAG

1. a
2. c
3. a
4. b
5. c
6. False
7. Mattel
8. b
9. False
10. False

YET ANOTHER GRAB BAG

1. False
2. False
3. True
4. True
5. True! What do *you* think—were they flattered or ticked off?
6. True
7. b
8. a
9. c
10. b

MIND-BLOWING TRIVIA CHALLENGE

1. b
2. a
3. b
4. a
5. c
6. b
7. Yellow
8. Gracie Films
9. 1987
10. b

THE SIMPSON HOME

1. A lamp and a phone.
2. False
3. b
4. False. It's an upright piano.
5. Yes
6. True
7. a
8. b
9. Yes
10. b
11. Yes
12. b
13. b
14. False
15. False

HELL #1

1. a
2. c
3. b
4. c
5. c
6. a
7. b
8. b. As proof, there are a slew of holes in a wall where a drunk Binky was trying to hang a picture of Sheba.
9. a
10. c

SPRINGFIELD

1. K-Babble
2. True
3. a
4. b
5. False
6. c
7. a

8. False
9. b
10. False

THE SCHOOL

1. Springfield Elementary
2. a
3. b
4. a
5. b (check the opening credits each week)
6. b
7. False
8. False

THE OPENING TITLES #1

1. False
2. P
3. Atomic symbols
4. b
5. False
6. False
7. a
8. Blue
9. a
10. True
11. Six
12. False
13. b
14. Matt Groening, natch!

CAN'T GET ENOUGH OF THOSE GRAB BAGS!

1: False
2. a
3. Burger King . . . which had nabbed the Teenage Mutant Ninja Turtles a few months before that. Either McDonald's has been snoozin' on the job . . . or they're afraid that the cowabunga dudes and caramba kid are a bit too wild for their image!

4. b
5. a
6. False
7. c
8. False
9. False

THE OPENING TITLES #2

1. c
2. a
3. False
4. c
5. False
6. False
7. False
8. Five
9. c
10. Black
11. c
12. c
13. False
14. c

HELL #2

1. c, d, g, and h
2. a
3. b
4. c
5. a

SOME EASY STUFF . . . AND SOME NOT-SO-EASY STUFF

1. b
2. False
3. That meticulous guardian of the public safety, Homer Simpson.
4. False
5. 555-PAIN

6. Bartman
7. c
8. False
9. False
10. c

ONE LAST GRAB BAG

1. False
2. b
3. b
4. a
5. c
6. a
7. Four
8. a
9. 8:30–9:00
10. Lisa

. . . EXCEPT FOR *THIS* GRAB BAG

1. b
2. c
3. False
4. a
5. b
6. True
7. False
8. c
9. False
10. False

WE MEAN IT, THIS REALLY *IS* THE LAST GRAB BAG . . .

1. Welcome is spelled Welcom on the first sign we see.
2. a
3. c
4. False
5. False
6. False

7. b
8. False
9. c
10. False

HOW POPULAR IS *THE SIMPSONS?*

From first place to tenth, here's how the characters and stars averaged out in our survey:
1. Bart Simpson
2. New Kids on the Block
3. Teenage Mutant Ninja Turtles
4. Super Mario Bros.
5. Arnold Schwarzenegger
6. Eddie Murphy
7. Batman
8. Chip 'n' Dale's Rescue Rangers
9. Paula Abdul
10. Pee-Wee Herman